Recharge your Batteries

How to optimize your energy and be at your best more often

Francesca Giulia Mereu

Foreword by Prof. Maury Peiperl

Illustrations by Harry Van Der Velde

" " To Artie Egendorf for his support and
trust that 'practice makes possible
long before it makes perfect' " "

Recharge your Spiritual Batteries

Conclusion

Bibliography

Preface

In my work with executives for over some 20 years, I have often found that, while an individual might have great strength in one or two resource areas, they would stand to benefit immensely from reflecting, and then acting, on the other key parts of the self. Indeed, it would not be an exaggeration to say that this has nearly always been the case. Those who have had this insight about themselves and acted on it have grown tremendously in their performance, their health, their self-confidence, and their satisfaction. Some of my closest friends and colleagues, as well as I myself, are examples.

Take the time to read this valuable book and to try the exercises it offers - you will surely find something here that will contribute significantly to your well-being, and through this, to your performance in whatever profession you dedicate yourself to as well as to the well-being and performance of those around you.

Maury Peiperl, PhD
Dean,
George Mason School of Business (USA)

Introduction

Introduction

Like most busy professionals, you know that your cell phone and laptop batteries must be charged regularly, but do you ever stop to think about recharging your own batteries?

- *Do you often feel exhausted by the end of your day?*

- *Do you aspire to have a much healthier lifestyle… yet struggle to change your habits?*

- *Do you find it difficult to wind down after a hard day's work and fully enjoy your personal life?*

- *Do you wonder if you will be able to keep up with your pace for the next five years?*

If you answered yes to any or all of these questions, then it is time to consider optimizing your energy level. This book is inspired in large from my own experience as a leadership coach.

Its very existence is largely thanks to the people who have tested, commented on, and applied the techniques that I have taught, for almost 20 years.

I facilitate seminars in different countries and in different professional circles. The participants themselves are very busy managers and leaders. My challenge has often been to provide tools for people who have busy schedules and little time to practice, yet require speedy results. The unique approach that I devised and tested with coachees, will also help those who want clear and achievable steps, with concrete ideas that quickly translate into practice.

Here are two goals you can achieve with this book:

1. *Increase your available energy level to reach your goals more easily and improve your quality of life – designed for long-term energy and during stressful times.*

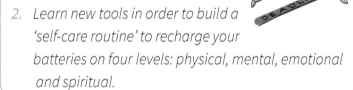

2. *Learn new tools in order to build a 'self-care routine' to recharge your batteries on four levels: physical, mental, emotional and spiritual.*

Work Life Balance

Put simply, it is a customized set of habits that help you sustain your energy level on a daily basis. A self-care routine prevents your batteries from getting too low, monitors your need to rest after a 'high', alerts you if are overusing or not using the same resources enough and generally increases your ability to bounce back and become yourself once more.

You can download a Self-Care Routine template from my website: www.pem.pm, found in the section, 'Try it out'.

We all have routines, habits and behaviors to care for our well-being. They may have worked once, but need to be regularly updated, just like software. Doing so will enable you to become your 'best self' by further building on your routine and finding important answers to questions, such as:

* *Do you have enough energy to match your needs, priorities and goals?*

* *How do your current habits support your quality of life?*

* *Contrary to this, do certain habits undermine or sabotage it?*

* *How could you recharge your batteries more often, even if you have little time to spare?*

Together, with the aid of this book, we will explore the four levels to further improve these dynamics:

1. *The physical level to optimize vitality and overall well-being.*

2. *The mental level to lead to more consistency and clarity between your thoughts and your actions.*

3. *The emotional level to channel your emotions and express them in a way that helps - not hinders - you.*

4. *The spiritual level to develop a strong motivation, deep-rooted in your values. This level refers to everything meaningful in your life, such as your passions, beliefs, and ethics - but not towards a particular religion!*

In reality, we are more than just the sum of four separate levels. We are a complex system where these four levels interact and create constantly. This model makes it easier to identify and structure how and when to act in order to optimize your energy levels.

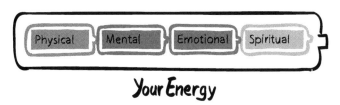

Your Energy

I would also like to clarify two words that you will often come across throughout this book: stress and resource. For the purposes of this book, the term stress is used as a synonym for blocked energy. The term resource means that this energy, once unblocked, may circulate freely in the four levels with noticeable benefits.

Here is an example which will help explain. You have just finished that all-important meeting that did not go so well and are still feeling frustrated. This frustration itself is a natural feeling. However, it can become a problem if it becomes lodged inside you and you find yourself dwelling on it instead of moving on, blaming yourself or others for the outcome. This is unhealthy. Your goal should be to regain access to your patience, your clarity or your focus - your inner resources. In this way you can learn, reflect and choose what you wish to do next.

The same is true if you had a great day, but it is now late at night and you need to reduce your adrenaline level in order to rest. What you need to do is to access your inner place of calm and tranquility. However, this takes a little practice. The key is to move easily from one state to the other. However, let me stress that it's not about denying the facts or fleeing from a problem. It's simply about observing, recognizing and finally accepting what is happening both inside us around us, and then responding more effectively.

In this case, 'more effectively' means that our decisions are based on a conscious decision that is better aligned with our objectives, and not upon an uncontrolled, scattered or random reaction. A feeling of fluidity and clarity emerges from this new approach. Imagine water that flows and takes to rough terrain while keeping its identity as water, allowing you to focus on the long term. Think in this way and you will start to understand the idea.

To help you take in and use these concepts effectively, these methods are depicted in the following two images:

impulse   outcome

When you are in a resourceful state, you are likely to feel that:

* You are comfortable in your mental and emotional space.

* You have a comfortable buffer. Imagine a large protective energy bubble constantly surrounding you – protecting you from negative thought which allows you to figure out calmly and clearly what to do next.

* Your actions are meaningful choices, conducive to reaching your goals and aligning with your values.

* You can easily access all your inner resources and feel that you have all the time you need.

* You are confident that you are able to deal with what happens without feeling the need to overreact.

In a nutshell, your imaginary bubble lets you feel and act like your 'best self'.

impulse   outcome

When you are in a stressed or blocked state for long periods of time, you are likely to feel that your actions are reactions:

- Scattered and only partially conducive to your goals.

- You are physically run down, mentally too wired or emotionally upset. Worse still, a mix of all three!

- You cannot access almost any of your inner resources and feel misaligned with your values.

- You feel low levels of control over yourself and the events that you are facing. People and situations seem to 'hit' you; they control your mood and ultimately control you.

Your imaginary buffer doesn't now seem so impenetrable. Your energy bubble is no longer a comfortable space in which to be. You neither feel nor act your 'best self'.

Noticing your energy bubble helps you to be your best self more often.

Throughout the day, your energy bubble constantly morphs: *it expands, it shrinks and it moves.* These changes are normal. What is important to know is how quickly and easily your bubble morphs back into a shape and size where you feel comfortable; and also what you can learn from these changes.

How is your bubble right now?

Notice its size, quality, color, sound, texture, smell or taste? Regularly check your bubble, notice the implications of its changes and decide what you are going to do about it!

You will find a chapter for each of the four levels of our energy: physical, mental, emotional and spiritual. Each chapter is divided into two main sections:

1. *Facts and ideas to explore. This section explains the models and ideas behind the tools that we will use.*

2. *Effective tools and techniques to try. This section describes the practices that my clients found most effective – and you will, too.*

In order to get the best out of this book, the mindset that I suggest you adopt is brilliantly summarized by this inspirational quote:

"Practice makes possible before it makes perfect"
Artie Egendorf. So, let's start this way!

Recharge your Physical Batteries

Why?

Facts and ideas to explore your physical energy

In this chapter I have presented simple, yet effective techniques for everyday use. Freeing blocked energy and releasing muscular micro-tensions helps us to be more relaxed at the end of the day and to have more energy overall. To better understand this, think of your body as a database. If you take the time to listen to what it is saying, it can provide you with information about your individual needs at different levels.

In this book, I define 'the body' as the tangible meeting point for our thoughts and emotions. If it is paid attention to and respected, it can contribute significantly towards increasing our vitality, clearing our thoughts and stabilizing our emotions.

Alarm   Resistance   Exhaustion

First of all, let's explore a few basic facts about stress and what we can learn from it. What actually is stress? Well, the term *stress*, as it is currently used, was first coined in 1936, by Hans Selye, who defined it as the non-specific response of the body to any demand for change. Now, stress is generally considered as negative as it is synonymous with *distress,* and is defined as "*a condition experienced when a person perceives that demands exceed the available personal and social resources necessary to cope with them.*" Yet, you may be surprised to learn that certain stress can, in fact, be beneficial when it motivates people to accomplish more. This is known as *eustress.* In this book I define stress as 'stuck or blocked energy', which we will learn to release and mobilize.

As defined by Hans Selye, here are the three phases of stress:

The alarm phase can be identified by a multitude of sensations. These can include an accelerated heart rate, short, quick breathing, clenched hands, sweating, goose bumps, etc. The nervous system is first to respond, by secreting the hormone *cortisol* and adrenaline responsible for all of these physiological factors.

Next, is the resistance phase which can manifest as light chronic tension (in the jaws, neck, shoulders, legs or elsewhere), a feeling of tightness when breathing, lumps in the throat, knots in the stomach, sweaty palms, a dry throat, indigestion or restlessness. It's difficult to be fully aware of this phase, as its physical manifestations are subtle, tolerable and have become familiar to us. It's the same as having a sore back, - it has become part of our internal landscape and we now are accustomed to it. It

doesn't prevent us from working, driving or even preparing a meal. Furthermore, given our hectic lifestyle, we simply convince ourselves that it's only a temporary discomfort or that it is no big deal. *"There are simply more important things."*

The exhaustion phase can happen at any time, with minimal or no apparent emotional or professional overload. At that time, everything more or less runs out: our ability to adapt, our physical resources and our emotional resilience to cope with changes, constraints and pressures. If our energy level decreases, it is more difficult to

enjoy our free time, to be able to work under pressure or to find pleasure in our relationship. Our health becomes affected: we may sleep less, tire quicker or even catch colds more frequently. That is why, when stress occurs, the body is the meeting point between thoughts, emotions and actions.

How is this relevant to our everyday life?

Imagine that after a long day at work, you have an evening with friends that was planned well in advance. As much as you are mentally looking forward it, your body is exhausted and you are fully aware that the following morning you will feel even more tired.

Physical fatigue often separates us from fully enjoying a pleasant experience. There are many possible ways to increase our responsibility towards our body, in the literal sense of the word 'response - ability': our ability to respond. Ways to respond may include carefully selecting foods that agree with us, exercising regularly, reducing alcohol and tobacco consumption, taking food supplements, and being mindful about the quality of our sleep, etc.

The various ways to support your body usually belong to three main areas: food, exercise and sleep - with sleep being the most important in terms of its impact on our food cravings, immune system, hormonal regulation and clarity of thinking.

I regularly observe that many of us are slightly or moderately sleep-deprived. If you are not entirely sure whether or not you suffer from a lack of sleep, ask yourself the following questions:

- *How is the quality of your sleep?*

- *Would you feel more rested if you went to bed a bit earlier?*

- *What could you do to rest more regularly? Would power napping be an option?*

- *Or is it your nutrition, or the amount of daily movement that would benefit from more attention?*

Your answers to these questions and subsequent decisions are individual choices and they take time and dedication.

This book focuses on easy to implement tools. I want to offer you faster ways to increase your energy level by identifying micro-tensions. Micro-tensions can be felt all over your body. It can be slightly tensed shoulders, jaws that clench when you feel anxious, frowning habitually, a tightness of your solar plexus, a sense of heaviness in the lower back, and so on.

They are not always painful and we are not necessarily aware of their presence, but they slowly tire us out, sapping our body of energy, making it more vulnerable to posture problems and often reduces our breathing capacity (along with the amount of oxygen available to the brain). It's a little like leaving the lights on when you leave your house. You will notice the impact only when you pay a much higher bill at the end of the month, with no extra benefit to you. If you make it part of your daily routine to consciously relax your entire body, you will immediately have more energy to direct to other areas or activities.

Assess

We all have parts of the body which are more sensitive than others and are the first to show signs of fatigue, such as the shoulders, jaws, hands, neck, back and chest.

* *Which are your specific sensitive areas?*

* *How can they let you know that you are experiencing stress or that you need a break?*

  – *Identify as many sensitive areas as you can and then choose one specific area to consciously monitor and actively relax during the day. Which parts of your body are the first to signal that you are feeling stressed or under pressure?*

  – *Observe where your body's vulnerable zones are. These are the areas that send you the early signals that you need a break. Which are they? Name them, remember them in your head and start to notice how they feel when you are starting to tire.*

- *It isn't difficult to do and the quicker you recognize these early signs, the easier it is to find a way to recharge or relax, like simply standing up and stretching for a couple of minutes.*

Act

Here is a simple series of movements that you could try. Before you do, assess your energy level on a scale from 1-10. Use this as a baseline so that you can check regularly if there is any change.

- *Contract every muscle from head to toe, no matter how you are positioned. Then relax them all at once by breathing out. Repeat this until you start to feel better. Usually, doing this 2 - 3 times will bring some relief. Now, re-assess your energy level.*

How is energy distributed?

To understand how energy is distributed, we will use different techniques inspired by Neuro-linguistic programming (NLP), a mental management method that provides a model for human behavior. According to the NLP Behavioral Model when we are focused and effective, our energy flows between three sectors:

- External Behaviors (EB), physical dimension.
  I blush …   I move …   I speak…

- Organization of Thoughts (OT), mental dimension.
  I think …   I structure …   I analyze…

- Internal States (IS), emotional dimension.
  I am calm …   I am angry …   I feel sad …

Behavioral Model based on NLP

So, our energy moves based on your thoughts, emotions and behaviors. According to this model, there is interdependence between the sectors: change something within one sector and the other two will also change. This is the theory, but on a daily basis, what could this imply in practice for you?

Here is a situation that should bring back memories for everyone: taking an exam. You know the material, you reviewed it well, and when you enter the room, you no longer know anything! Just the same, you answer questions, you sweat, perhaps you pray to a higher power for help, and when leaving, you tell yourself that you have failed. According to the interdependence model, here is what happened: all of your energy moved to your feelings (IS, fear) and you no longer had enough to think (OT, you confuse two words). As for your external behavior (EB), it also underwent some changes: you were sweating and were likely flushed.

Now think back to the last time you were at the dentist. You're sitting in the dreaded chair, trying to reassure yourself about what's going to happen to you. Suddenly, you realize that you are gripping the armrests tightly with your fingers. Then almost as quickly, you loosen your grip and almost instantly, a wave of relaxation comes over you and you feel better. What happened? About 80% of your energy went to the external behavior (EB).

Your clenched fingers sent an alarm message to your brain (OT), which put you in a state of stress (IS). Yet, when you release the pressure from your fingers (EB), you calmed down (IS) and you felt a little better (OT).

All learning passes through the senses. Put simply, this means that if we see, hear, and/or feel a situation, we will have either good or bad memories when a similar situation occurs. These memories will, in turn, affect how we choose to behave. If we are feeling confident and at ease, the likelihood is that, we are able to handle and respond better to situations with all our resources.

Examples of how our senses affect our behaviors are a song, a barking dog, or a particular place. Depending on your personal experience, you will listen to the song with more or less enjoyment, you will hesitate to pat the neighbor's dog, and you may avoid the place you are thinking about, etc. The role of this mental imagery is fundamental in facilitating changes, overcoming difficult moments and being able to self-motivate.

Since we are using NLP as a model, it would be useful to understand a little more about its history. Linguist John Grinder and mathematician Richard Bandler developed this method in California in the 1970s. They first met at the University of California, in Santa Cruz, where they both studied psychology and discovered that they shared a common curiosity on the theme of knowledge and raised a number of questions. How do we learn? How do we share our knowledge? How do we change? Above all, how can we learn and change faster? To answer these questions, a group of young likeminded researchers joined them, namely Leslie Cameron, Judith

DeLozier, David Gordon and Robert Dilts. Everyone had similar interests in the transfer of knowledge, but with different focuses: on emotions, therapeutic metaphors or neurophysiology. Their research was based on observation of the entire branch of psychology in general, and the direct study of three exceptional communicators and therapists: Fritz Pearl, Milton Erickson and Virginia Satir. The basic question was: *What differentiates an excellent professional from an average professional?*

The answer was based upon the abilities of these therapists (and others) to piggyback on their patients' behavior. This is known as *synchronization.* Following this observational work, the researchers found a series of techniques which enabled them to *model excellence*. This is analyzing a behavioral structure and quickly reproducing a method, a performance or a skill.

NLP also explores our communication style and the way that we interpret and describe events in our lives.

We have an innate tendency - of animal origin - to prefer people we perceive as being similar to ourselves. For this reason, we communicate better if we adjust our speech rate and movements to match those around us. To bond we either seek similarity or create it. It's not about imitating the other, but to match with elegance. Furthermore, we do it spontaneously when we are comfortable with the people around us. In a group or pair, if a person crosses the legs or the arms, the others are likely to do a similar gesture. Conversely, if you are sitting straight in your chair and your partner is leaning back, this is known as *mismatching* in NLP jargon. It is very useful when you wish to end the conversation and leave. You can see this everywhere: in restaurants, offices, on the train, etc. Try it for yourself. Have a little fun observing the matching or *mismatching* postures, including your own.

NLP allows us to recondition the behaviors that increase our well-being, to channel our resources to where we have decided they are the most useful and to reduce self-sabotaging behaviors. Our physical resources, therefore, also influence our emotions and our thoughts. And if we had trouble sleeping, we are more irritable, our reasoning is slower, we feel disconnected from the rest of the world, and so on.

External Behaviors are strongly connected with our Physical Energy.

34

How?
Tools and techniques to try out

Together, we will now explore new techniques to add to your habitual ones and help you build your routine of self-care. There are four simple yet highly effective routines that you can use during the day:

1. *Two-Minute Tip*

2. *Target Booster*

3. *Static Booster*

4. *Aligned Posture*

Remember, we are a whole, so no matter which technique you try, it will positively affect all the four levels of your energy: physical, mental, emotional and spiritual.

Before you start, let's examine the benefits of each tool.

The benefits of Target and Static Boosters

The objective of this series of movements is to identify and target the tensions and tightness in your muscles that absorb energy and slowly tire your body. These simple movements do not replace regular exercise, but instead relax the micro-tensions in a short period of time and with minimal effort. Any office job where you sit at your desk all day, amplify these micro-tensions that turn into pain in the cervical vertebrae, stiffness in the shoulders and fatigue in the wrists (carpal tunnel syndrome, caused by poor positioning when handling a computer mouse).

Importantly, pay close attention to your posture while you work. You may be surprised, but this is much more beneficial to your back than going to the gym three times a week. When we work, we are very often seated, hence the importance of holding yourself both upright and comfortable. Preferably sit with your feet flat on the ground, your arms and forearms relaxed, jaw loosened, and of course, your spine straight, without being too rigid. Ultimately, the basic idea is to find the most comfortable position combined with the most economical for your muscles, depending upon the context. You will end up noticing how much your posture also impacts your mental and emotional resources.

Body Influence

Try this exercise to understand how your body influences your thoughts and your emotions.

body influences

- *For 30 seconds, sit with your head between your hands, looking at the ground, with your shoulders turned inward and your eyebrows furrowed. Stand up and stretch.*

- *Then, for the next 30 seconds sit up straight, look off into the distance, relax your face and shoulders and smile slightly.*

What did you feel, see, and hear in the first, closed position? How was it different when in the second, open position? What degree of comfort or discomfort did you have? Notice how changing your physiology (even when done artificially), affects how you feel and how you think.

When you are more aware of your posture, you save energy by optimizing the way you move. For example, you are likely to reduce or stop gestures like frowning and clenching your jaws while writing, or contorting your entire body to open a jar of pickles. Tell yourself: If you hold your pen too firmly or your shoulders higher than necessary, these are typical indicators of stress.

Another example while driving, we often grip the steering wheel too tightly with far more strength than needed, frown and sometimes breathe faster. These are telltale signs that we are upset, anxious or worried. If you are able to notice these signs and relax your body to conserve your physical energy, you can channel it where you need it the most.

But what if your day flew by at lightning speed, without having had the time, or the reflex, to stop for a moment's respite, in order to practice the little exercises you have learned? Setbacks like this are normal in any change process. Research has shown that new habits can take anywhere from three weeks to six months before becoming second nature, provided it is repeated regularly each day. So be patient with yourself and use the suggestions to relax in the evening for example. Start the process early in the evening or before going out or just before going to bed.

A good idea is to choose just one technique or idea to try out per chapter, so that you end up with one 'mini-habit' - an action that is meaningful yet is so small and so easy that you can't fail to do it. It could be as simple as going to bed 10 minutes earlier than usual, doing three minutes stretching a day, drinking one glass of water more...

Here are two examples of mini-habits to help you relax your body during the day:

* Standing, with your legs spread apart, slowly lift then lower your arms like a bird.

* Sitting comfortably, make small circular motions with your head.

Focus on your movements and maintain a regular breathing rhythm: try breathing a little deeper and a little slower than your usual pace. This will help create a *mental*

silence for a few minutes while increasing the benefits of the movements.

Whether standing or sitting, observe your sensitive areas and relax them with some simple movements such as stretching or contracting and relaxing them. Add the breathing as in the previous exercise.

The benefits of an aligned posture

How many times were you told when you were young (and even afterwards) *"Sit up straight… don't slouch so much… behave yourself!"* You may associate correct posture to a constraint, to a feeling of military discipline, to a rigid mental attitude or to cold, formal behavior. However, there are at least two benefits to an aligned posture: (1) your movements are more economical from an energy point of view; and (2) it takes you less effort to accomplish your daily tasks, such as standing, sitting, driving, walking and eating.

If abdominal breathing (see Chapter 2 about mental resources) increases your vitality by providing more oxygen, an aligned posture helps you to reduce waste. Note that a straight posture begins with a flexible spinal column! In the United Kingdom, 12.5% of sick leave is related to back problems. This figure demonstrates the seriousness of this problem. Breathing also keeps the spine flexible, stretching it very slightly as you breathe in and out. These little induced movements are crucial. If the spine loses its flexibility, it in turn reduces the magnitude of breathing and makes muscular contraction in the back, the shoulders and the neck more likely. The muscles shorten and/or weaken which hinders the whole mechanism.

C. Hauser-Bischof stated: "*A posture is considered as normal when an adequately mobile spinal cord can be maintained in the upright position for hours, with minimal muscular contribution*". This posture requires that your balance is dynamic, constantly adjusting with very little movement. It also depends on the flexibility and length of your muscles. This results in energy savings in all of your actions and movements.

The goal of the following techniques is to mobilize your spine gently, using practices that you can do in the comforts of your own home. If you then decide to work more with your posture, I suggest that you explore four mobilization methods that have a solid background backed by years of studies: Rolfing, Feldenkreis, Alexander and Pilates. However, check with your doctor if you think it's necessary.

1. Two-Minute Tip

When you travel on an airplane, you probably will notice that the airline companies recommend that passengers do little exercises during the flight. These simple exercises include getting up from time to time, moving your feet and calves, moving your shoulders, stretching and so on. They can also be done at your place of work when you are sitting for hours at a time.

- *If you work for long periods in the same position (sitting down or standing), give yourself two minutes of targeted relaxation every hour - see how quickly you will start to feel better at the end of the day.*

2. Target Booster

After you wake up, spend 2-3 minutes (or 4-5 minutes during the day) to find a quiet place where you can remove your shoes and be alone.

- *Stand in a comfortable position. Evaluate your current energy level on a scale of 1 to 10.*

  Begin by observing your body. Identify which area(s) are currently tense - they are the ones you will be working on (see below). If you have already identified other sensitive areas, treat them in the same way!

When you have finished, evaluate your energy level again and compare it with how you felt at the beginning.

General areas to relax

Around the eyes: Massage around your eyes by making little circles or close your eyes and press your fingers above your eyebrows, from the center of your face outwards.

Neck: Tilt the weight of your head forward and turn it slowly and gently from one side to the other. Also, relax your jaw and take deeper and slower breaths than usual.

Jaw: Press the two junction points of the mandible and massage with circular movements. Yawn to relax the diaphragm and to ease your breathing.

Shoulders: Roll both your shoulders forwards and backwards, while focusing on your movement or your breathing. To facilitate concentration, place the opposite hand on the shoulder that you are moving.

Lower back: With your hands on your hips, make a circle with your pelvis in one direction, then the other. Focus on the movement itself and not on the magnitude. Flexibility comes with practice.

Feet: Shift your weight back and forth while pressing your toes and heels into the ground.

Check again your energy level and notice if the level has changed.

Post practice comments

Patience is everything! In the beginning, it may not be easy to determine your energy level. With experience, however, you will start to get a better feel for the changes in your vitality and muscle tone. Also, learn to lower the volume of your internal dialogue. This is that voice in your head that speaks about an overpriced bill while we are driving, that counts the days before Christmas in the middle of July, and makes us think about the Caribbean while we are at work. If this voice returns during the exercises, use your bubble and focus more on your senses: your movements, your breathing, or even the texture of your clothing. Sometimes, your tensions will feel stronger, but don't worry as this is normal. The movement and focus will release blocked energy as it awakens. However, if you notice persistent physical tensions, you might want to consult a professional. *Remember: observe, recognize and accept what your body is telling you.*

3. Static Booster

These two variations have the same goals as the Target Booster: to increase your flexibility and prevent the accumulation of physical blockages and associated fatigue.

- *Shift your attention to the following zones and relax the appropriate muscles as soon as you notice tension:*
  - *Your face, eyebrows, forehead and jaw.*
  - *Your neck, shoulders and back.*
  - *Your hands and fingers.*
  - *Your breathing... the stomach, chest, buttocks.*
  - *Your knees and feet.*
  - *Your specific areas (the ones you've identified).*

You should start to notice and even enjoy how the different areas feel when you do this.

- *This technique will help you fall asleep better if you do it when you go to bed. To make it more effective, visualize your fatigue and unpleasant thoughts and let them go when you breathe out. We will revisit the mechanisms and benefits of visualization in* Chapter 3, *which is about emotional resources. In the beginning, use this method while you are lying on your back, in bed, on the sofa, or even on the ground - you just need to be comfortable. Start by breathing in and pointing your toes forward for*

two seconds, then contract your muscles and relax them when breathing out. Shift your focus to the following areas (again contract your muscles as you breathe in and relax them as you breathe out):

- *Your legs... your buttocks...*
- *Open and close your fingers...*
- *Your arms...*
- *Rotate and relax your shoulders...*
- *Stretch your neck, make faces, furrow your eyebrows...*
- *Contract your entire body and then let go.*

Repeat if you wish. Then think of a happy cat stretching on his favorite cushion and move in a way that feels good for you. Take your time and enjoy this relaxing feeling as long as you wish. Then, at your own pace, and start moving your hands and feet. Next, turn on your right side and get up slowly (or stay lay down and enjoy a peaceful sleep).

Always start this sequence on the same side, or with the same part of your body, it will help to anchor it in yourself. Your body and mind will remember that a certain contraction generates a series of movements ending in a relaxed, comfortable state. Give yourself time to become familiar with the various parts of your body.

When you use these techniques during the day, evaluate your energy level at the beginning and at the end and then observe the effects. What are the benefits? Does it feel energizing, relaxing or soothing?

You can do these movements even if you are sitting in your office or during the day if you want to have a mini-break or shift focus. Of course, the best thing is to get up and change environment for the 2 - 4 minute exercises. If this is not possible, simply move your legs, abdominal and buttock muscles (or less visible places) and breathe out discreetly. No one needs to know that you're recharging your batteries. Think about this any time you need to recharge but can't physically move. It could be during a key meeting, if you are stuck in a traffic jam or even if you are struggling to concentrate when writing emails.

4. Aligned Posture

The best time to practice this is when you wake up in the morning or at night before going to bed. Lay on your back, on the ground or other firm place. As before, evaluate your energy level on a scale from 1 to 10.

• *Place your arms along your sides, palms facing the ground. Stretch your neck slightly upward and tuck in your chin a little. Carefully stretch backward.*

Spread your feet about 40 cm apart and bend your legs; find the right distance that feels comfortable.

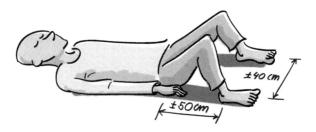

Your heels should be about 50 cm from your buttocks and your entire back should be touching the ground.

Very slowly, roll your pelvis upward, thus rounding the lower vertebrae and the lower back (you can lift your pelvis a little to make the movement easier). Keep your arms relaxed on the ground and breathe normally.

Return your back to the ground, unrolling it vertebra by vertebra (this is only an intention, otherwise the movement is very difficult to do literally), relax your legs and the muscles in your buttocks and breathe softly.

Repeat this motion two more times, going further up your spine each time and do it until you feel you wish to stop.

Stop and take a break, stretch out your legs, relax your shoulders, neck, fingers and hands.

Do another cycle of three movements: small, medium and larger ones.

With practice, you will find the number of repetitions that suits you. The movements are fluid, soft and slow, your focus is on the controlled rolling of your spine and on the enjoyment of stretching. At your own pace, stretch and stand back up (think about the cat from the preceding exercise). Evaluate your energy level again and feel the difference in your body.

Post practice comments

Be patient if you have difficulty rocking your pelvis and rolling upwards. Our Western culture tends to discourage undulations of the pelvis and relegate them to dance. To inspire your movement, think of the image *vertebra by vertebra* and focus on the controlled unwinding of your spine. Sometimes, other muscles will involuntarily contract during your concentration. It will help if you breathe slowly, relax your arms and smile slightly. You body's needs also change every day. Some days you will feel like focusing more on certain areas and others on different ones. Listen to the messages and use your body as a data bank.

- *How is your back now?*

- *Do you feel more flexible, more aware and more mobile?*

- *Do you notice any changes? Any discomfort? If you feel aching, it's because you forced yourself to do too much. Relax, and next time, you will be able to better listen to your body and respect its current limits.*

- *Avoid doing this exercise on a bed, unless it is very firm like a futon. Often, a soft carpet or a thick towel on the floor are better options.*

Conclusion

Observe your body, recognize the areas that are more sensitive to stress and accept their messages. This is how you will learn to optimally use your physical energy and be able to implement sustainable changes. You have all the necessary resources to discover your unique energetic balance. Remember that the mental, physical and emotional levels are interdependent. You now know more techniques to revitalize, relax your body and release blocked energy (which we defined as stress). Create a routine that suits you, start by perfecting one technique, be patient with what you discover and with the pace of your changes.

In my experience, it is better to start with small changes, small new habits, so small that you can't fail them - no matter how tired or busy you are. It may be one stretch in the morning, it may be two rounds of abdominal breathing a day or it may be one walk a week. Trust that these tiny steps will compound and create a snowball effect.

Recharge your Mental Batteries

Why?
Facts and ideas to explore your mental energy

Physical resources are easy to identify when they are drained because they are connected to our health and overall vitality. They are also straightforward to measure through our breathing patterns, hours of sleep, glucose levels, heart rates and so on. On the other hand, mental resources, such as focus, decision making, the ability to analyze, and processing complex information, are less clearly measured and are strongly affected by the physical, emotional and spiritual levels. Nevertheless, this differentiation helps you to notice what requires your attention and makes it easier and quicker to rebalance your energy levels. We define mental resources as our ability to align our thoughts and decisions with our goals and actions.

And as we saw with the Behavioral Model, the synergy of the three sectors ensures the best results. This synergy is also based on the power of consistency.

Behavioral Model
The Organization of Thought is strongly
connected with our Mental Energy

Consistency aligns mental energy with behaviors and emotions, similarly to how correct posture aligns physical energy. To understand this more easily, try imagining someone giving you good news with an angry facial expression or someone thanking you warmly using very formal words. This would be somewhat perplexing to most of us, and you would find the message - or the person - less convincing. Now think of the power of a clear idea, rooted in our values and expressed with appropriate voice and gestures. Consistency reinforces the meaning that we give to our actions and it's in the search for meaning where we, as humans, find the source of its deepest energy.

The *'why?'* that we attribute to our choices and events gives us the ability to see things either as opportunities or as problems. We will revisit this theme in the chapters relating to emotional resources (Chapter 3) and spiritual resources (Chapter 4).

Two models of the brain

For about 20 years now, brain researchers have made enormous progress thanks to technological advancement. For example, brain activity can now be measured with extreme precision using an MRI (magnetic resonance imaging). Discoveries in neuropsychology show that the brain's chemical balance directly impacts our internal state (IS). The lines between the physical, intellectual and emotional are slowly disappearing, which has helped create a map showing which part of the brain is activated in response to specific tasks or emotions.

A widely popular model attributes to the two halves of our brain - the left and the right hemispheres - different functions.

- The left hemisphere primarily controls the functions of calculation and analysis, sequences, language, attention to detail and temporal perspective (past-present-future), it uses linear reasoning and tends to understand things literally.

- The right hemisphere is mainly responsible for the bigger picture, of movements in space, rhythm and perception and focuses more on the present moment. It treats this information in a more holistic way and uses metaphors.

We will also use the theory that we have a dominant hemisphere - in the same way we have a dominant hand - and when we are under stress we are more likely to shift to that hemisphere, thus losing access to the skills of the other one. For example, you might notice that when you are upset, you tend to talk more or to talk less (but still feel a lot), to focus on the details or just look at the bigger picture and so on. These are all signs of a possible preference.

More than just being divided into two hemispheres, the brain is a layered structure. Neurologist Paul D. McLean first proposed this theory in the 1960s and called it the *triune brain*, meaning *three in one*.

- The first brain, or the reptilian brain, is the deepest part and the oldest in terms of evolution. Its name derives from the fact that this structure is similar to the one that fish and reptiles have. It controls the body's vital functions, such as breathing, heartbeat, temperature and so on.

- Then there is the limbic brain, which is found above the first. Researchers consider it as an area that modifies the instinctual behaviors generated by the underlying layer. Its first task is to guarantee the survival of the individual or the animal. The limbic brain controls and modulates impulses (eating, drinking and sexuality, etc.) and shows increased activity during periods of strong emotions. It activates in stressful situations and tells us, for example, to run if we are in danger, to fight or freeze if we cannot run.

- In mammals that have most recently developed, like us *Homo sapiens*, the third layer of the brain is the thickest and is known as the neocortex. The folds of the neocortex increase its surface, resulting in a greater number of neurons. The frontal lobe of the neocortex - and more specifically the pre-frontal lobe - is the area activated when we plan, think, create and imagine and so on. Yet this area is not as active when we experience strong emotions, such as fear, anxiety or anger. Conversely, in this same situation, MRIs have shown that there is very strong activity in the limbic brain and the reptilian brain.

To better visualize the different areas of the brain, you can watch this excellent seven-minute video, by Daniel Siegel, professor at UCLA in Los Angeles: https://goo.gl/mxLBs6.

What can we take away from these models?

Becoming more aware of what supports your brain's functions and being able to access both your hemispheres - especially when you feel stressed - is a great asset to access all your mental resources.

In this chapter we will explore the benefits of three simple yet successful techniques (the movements of the Brain Gym®, abdominal breathing and mental imagery) that will allow you to shift your focus more easily between the hemispheres and tap into the power of your neocortex.

Benefits of the Brain Gym®

> "Mix clay into a pot,
> it is the emptiness inside
> that makes it useful"
> – *Tao Te King*

Similarly to a clay pot, our mind loses its effectiveness when it is totally full. Studies have shown that on average our concentration decreases after 40-60 minutes of focused work. However, should you take a break for a few minutes within this timeframe, it will help you regain your focus faster. On the other hand, the longer we wait for this break, the more time it will take to recover our concentration. If we

Each 40-60 minutes

learn to recognize and listen to our physiological rhythms and know our personal differences, we can make our intellectual performance more stable and prevent the mind from *going blank*. The Brain Gym® method will help you increase your attention span and regain your focus faster.

This method was developed by American psychologist, Paul Dennison, in the 1970s. In the beginning, his goal was to help children with learning difficulties. This method is derived from kinesiology, which shares its theoretical bases with human biology, neurophysiology and Chinese medicine.

There are around twenty movements in total and were designed specifically for children. Their names are easy to memorize and to execute and are quickly effective. Little by little, Brain Gym® practitioners realized that these exercises might also be suitable for adults who wish to maintain their concentration and focus when they were working long hours or needed to keep a clear head for decision making.

Brain Gym® supports the idea discussed in the previous section about a dominant hemisphere - in the same way we have a dominant hand, eye or leg. It's similar to being left or right-handed. When the brain is at rest without any particular emotion, we draw from the resources of the entire brain, both left and right hemispheres, and especially the pre-frontal lobe. Conversely, when we are tired or experiencing strong emotions, our dominant hemisphere and the posterior parts of the brain (limbic and reptilian) take over, triggering strong emotions, such as fight or flight. It is important to understand this predominance in order to better manage our reactions during times of stress.

Exercises to Determine Your Dominant Hemisphere

- *Stand up comfortably. Shift your weight to one leg without thinking about which side, just do it.*

  Your dominant hemisphere is very likely the opposite of the leg supporting your weight.

  The second possibility is to ask yourself what you like to do during your free time. If you prefer to read

a book or do crossword puzzles, you are left-brained. Alternatively, if you prefer to draw or play music, you are more likely right-brained.

Reflection: When you have a problem, do you prefer to analyze it, describe it with specific words or even write it down? This indicates a dominant left brain. In contrast, when you experience emotions, do you consider the situation a problem in the big picture? Do you feel the need to move, take a walk to think about it? If so, your right brain is dominant. Remember that the concept of a dominant hemisphere is just that - a concept - and not a proven scientific fact. The interest of it is to help you understand your *self* better through different theoretical frameworks.

For example, when we feel stressed, a predominance of the right brain may cause us to see only the overall vision and forget the small details. In addition, language skills stem from the left brain, so we might experience difficulty in formulating thoughts or finding the right words to express ourselves when we are upset.

So, how can we keep accessing all the parts of our brain when we are under pressure?

Here's how to reestablish and maintain communication between both hemispheres. Consider setting 2- to 5-minute breaks for yourself once an hour or every 45 minutes. Just take your nose away from the monitor, stretch and do the following exercises. Each exercise will help you in a different way. However, before trying them out, prepare yourself by first doing these Three Pre-Activities:

- *I.   Sitting or standing, extend an arm in front of you, parallel to the ground and lift the index and the middle finger. Without moving your head, follow your fingers with your eyes while making a circle with your arm, as wide as possible while still seeing your fingers. Follow your fingers up, down, to the right or to the left. Notice where it is easier and where it is less smooth. Change arms and direction and repeat the same movement.*

- *II. Read a one-page text (something you're with familiar or not).*

read one page

65

- *III. Stand with your feet together and*  *legs straight, then lean forward. Take note of how far you can go, without forcing yourself. Simply notice how far your hands can go: do they touch your knees, your ankles, or the ground?*

Once you have finished, begin the exercises which I will describe later

(see How? – Tools and techniques to try out).

Benefits of abdominal breathing

Our breathing varies according to our environment and how we perceive it. Abdominal breathing is controlled in part by the abdominal muscles. However, a specific muscle controls these variations: the diaphragm. The diaphragm enables us to laugh, yawn, sigh, and, even something less pleasant: hiccups. The diaphragm is what spasms  when we have those annoying hiccups. It's a muscle that separates the lungs from the abdomen and it can be compared to an umbrella that opens when lowering and closes when rising.

The diaphragm flattens when inhaling and relaxes when exhaling. Abdominal breathing (or diaphragmatic) means to fill the bottom of the lungs, versus thoracic (chest) breathing which uses the middle part, and sub-clavicular breathing that moves the upper portion. Abdominal breathing is characteristic in children, those who play wind instruments, singers and athletes.

In stressful situations, our breathing speeds up and also loses amplitude, which results in a sensation of a lack of oxygen, fullness or tightness in the chest, or a closed-up feeling. It's a truly vicious circle, but one that can be reversed. If we first control our breathing, we can calm our mental state, impacting the physical state, which, in turn will eventually calm the psychological state.

Finally, you may be surprised to know, but it is impossible to get angry when breathing calmly and deeply, using the abdominal breathing method!

Abdominal Breathing

To experience this concept in your body, you can try this:

- *When you are breathing deeply, think of something that greatly upsets you, not a traumatic one, just something*

that makes you angry. You'll notice that it is much more difficult to feel angry, compared to when you think of the same situation and breathe normally.

Your physiology does not support your emotions and in turn reduces their intensity.

- *Conversely, when you are relaxed, speed up and shorten your breaths. You will soon notice a slight feeling of anxiety or reduced mental clarity that has nothing to do with any facts or real situation.*

- *Return to your normal breathing and complete two rounds of abdominal breathing to calm down again.*

A note about abdominal breathing

Even though thoracic breathing (filling the mid part of the lungs) is the most widespread method used by Western adults, abdominal breathing, as a result of its depth, is the most effective way to thoroughly oxygenate our bodies.

To give you an idea of what good oxygenation is, our brain alone consumes 25% of all the oxygen we absorb, although it represents only 2% of the body's total weight. The results are easy to see and feel. More oxygen means more vigor, more physical and intellectual endurance and less drowsiness. Deeper breathing also increases movement of the diaphragm and indirectly massages the internal organs. It helps with digestion, relaxes tension in the back and promotes intestinal transit.

A final effect of abdominal breathing, which is observed through MRI, is to shift our mental activity from the limbic system again to the 'cooler' and more creative pre-frontal cortex, which is extremely useful when we are perturbed or derailed by intense emotions.

Benefits of NLP visualization to optimize your effectiveness

Have you ever stayed awake all night because something keeps running through your mind? Have you ever thought about a past situation as if it were there, in front of you?

If you answered 'Yes' then you know visualization. Channel this ability: mental images, when positive, enable you to improve your performance by using mental repetition of the desired behavior. This is the way athletes train themselves. Visualization increases their concentration during competition, as well as the precision of their movements and resistance to stress.

Likewise, have you ever heard music that brought you back to a particular time in your life associated with it or tasted a meal that reminded you of your childhood? Again, if you answered, *'Yes,'* then you know about anchoring. Anchoring, often done unconsciously, connects an internal state (the strength of memory and emotions) to a movement, sound, image, smell or taste.

By creating conscious anchors, we learn to voluntarily link a positive internal state (safety, peace, confidence) to a movement, image, sound or situation. This is useful in order to trigger that positive internal state when you are feeling uneasy. NLP uses this technique to mobilize all of our senses and to integrate a new behavior more quickly. We all have a sensory preference when analyzing and perceiving a situation. Some recall what they have *seen*, others recall what they have *heard* or *felt*.

In NLP terms, you activate either, your visual, auditory or kinesthetic channel more, depending on your preference in processing information. *Do you know if you have a preferred channel? Well, it is very easy to find out. Simply think about a film that you saw recently and start to describe it. Then notice which words you choose: do you notice a majority of words related to visual cues (images, color, scene), or acoustic cues (the music, the special effects) or to kinesthetic cues (how it felt: gripping, inspiring, thrilling, soothing, or funny)? This will help you find your preferred*

channel. Knowing this will help you integrate key words into your visualizations, mental training and self-motivation. The more you are able to mobilize your senses, the easier it is to act as you choose.

This is advantageous when you are in an unpleasant situation that may be repeated, known as the present state. You then want to improve this situation

so that it no longer bothers you. This is called the desired state. For example, if you are afraid of driving - present state - you can anchor the concept of *driving confidence* - desired state - before getting into your car. Make a fist and tell yourself: "*This car feels comfortable and safe. It looks solid or it sounds very reliable, and I'll be fine!*" You can make this a habit by making a fist along the way. This gesture will remind you that you have implemented the concept and a feeling of confidence and you can relax. The more you use conscious anchoring, the more effective it will be in all circumstances.

If you use this technique in different situations, just be careful not to put all the anchor points at the same part of your body, otherwise you may mix everything up!

If you don't know which place to use for your anchoring point, you can just as easily choose where you wear a ring, a pendant or a watch.

There is no specific duration for this visualization exercise. You may be very quick or very slow, but that's not important. However, you will know better than anyone when you are ready to create your anchor point and how to use it. At first, this technique might be easier for those who are visual, who will represent events with images or films. If you 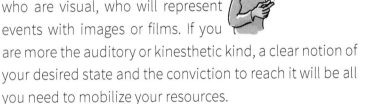 are more the auditory or kinesthetic kind, a clear notion of your desired state and the conviction to reach it will be all you need to mobilize your resources.

So, what do you want in the end? If it's to be more confident when driving (desired state), make sure it's what you *really* want. Use the following six criteria to double-check the feasibility of your desired state:

Personal: Who does it depend on? *On you, only you! Not on the actions of somebody else.*

Possible and realistic: What have you already achieved that was similar? How can you frame it in a way that it feels possible, while taking into account your present state and starting point?

Positive: Think about what you want, instead of what you want to avoid.

Verifiable and observable: How do you know that it's what you want? What will be the signs that you are succeeding? What are your indicators?

Contextual: When and where do you want to achieve your goals? Think about your timeline and specific situations.

Ecological: Is it acceptable? Is it worth taking your values and the bigger picture into consideration?

Note that these six criteria are extremely useful in structuring any goal, any time!

After checking these points, you might need to redefine your desired state. Once you find it and it clearly expresses your intention, start visualizing.

If disruptive thoughts arise, return your focus gently and firmly to the process and continue the exercise.

Your goal has to depend on your actions and behaviors.

You are the one who owns the choice and the definition of your goal and your desired state. Of course, finding support to implement it is another essential step.

How?
Tools and techniques to try out

You will now have the chance to experience first-hand, three techniques and decide which one works best for you:

1. *Brain Gym®*

2. *Abdominal Breathing*

3. *NLP Visualization*

Please remember that we are very much a unique system, so these techniques are likely to balance your emotions and your physical well-being, too.

1. Brain Gym® Exercises

Let's recall the three pre-activities:

- *I. While sitting or standing,*  *extend an arm in front of you, parallel to the ground, and lift the index and the middle finger. Without moving your head, follow your fingers with your eyes while making a circle with your arm, as wide as possible while still looking at your fingers. Follow your fingers up, down, to the right or to the left, notice where is easier and where it is less smooth. Change arms and direction and repeat the same movement.*

II. Read a one-page text (that you may or  *may not be familiar with).*

III. Stand with your feet together and legs straight, and lean forward.

read one page

Look how far you can go, without forcing yourself. Look at how far your hands can go. Do they touch the knees, the ankles, or even the ground?

Now, you are ready for the following exercises:

The Cross Crawl activates both cerebral hemispheres simultaneously. The brain better coordinates the processing of visual, auditory and kinesthetic (related to bodily sensations) information. This improves listening, reading and memory.

- *Standing, touch your left knee with your right hand and vice-versa. Start to slowly and gradually increase the rhythm. Length: at least seven times on each side.*

The Energy yawn: Amazingly, almost 50% of neurological connections between the brain and the rest of the body go through the joints of the jaws! Massaging these areas relaxes them, frees the connections and improves exchanges between the two hemispheres.

- *Massage the junction point of the jaws, relax your eyebrows and your mouth during the exercise and yawn as much as you can.*

The Lazy Eight integrates visual fields (right and left) and promotes balance and concentration. This exercise, done through relaxing the eyes, enables you to absorb visual information easier or to better concentrate when writing.

- *Standing, with your legs spread about shoulder width apart, clasp your hands in front of you. Now trace an imaginary lazy 8 (horizontally) with your hands, remembering to go up - not down - every time you come back to center. Look at your hands without moving your head. Make the movements as sweeping and calm as you can and the weight of your body should go from right to left with your knees bent. Length: at least 7 lazy eights or as many as you wish.*

The **Listening Flaps** reduces disruptive noise and promotes listening to rhythms, such as music or the spoken word. According to Chinese medicine, there are many areas on our ears that correspond to the major organs.

- *Massage your ears with both hands. Simply pull them up, down and to the sides. Do this for about 30 seconds.*

The Brain Buttons are those of acupressure, known to activate the brain's frontal lobe, reduce emotional stress and focus attention.

- *Place one hand 2-3 cm from your navel. Simultaneously, with your other hand, massage the two points underneath your collar bone. These points are about 10 cm from one another. Switch hands. Do this exercise for about 30 seconds and then switch hands again.*

Repeat the three pre-activities and compare the results (for the reading activity, find a new text). You will notice that it is useless repeating the exercises too much and for too long. Follow your instinct! With practice, you will know what your ideal duration is.

2. Abdominal Breathing

The technique we have chosen comes from *Pranayama* (from Sanskrit, meaning *science of breathing*), which is a branch of *Hatha Yoga*, the physical branch of the Indian philosophy of Yoga Vedanta.

Open a window, go out on the balcony, or better still, go outdoors - but only if you are near a garden or a park. Find a place to sit down comfortably and close your eyes to encourage concentration.

- *Keep your back and head straight, as if they were suspended with a thread. Let your shoulders drop down, relax your fingers, your wrists and your jaw. Place one hand 2-3 cm under your navel and breathe normally.*

- *After three or four breaths, exhale a little longer than usual: your breathing will automatically become deeper.*

- *Keep your breathing smooth, with your jaw and shoulders relaxed. Continue exhaling a little longer than normal. You should notice that your breathing is now deeper.*

- *As soon as you feel the warmth of your hand on your stomach, imagine that you are guiding the breath to this area. Continue this for a half dozen breaths. With practice you will find your optimal number of rounds.*

- *To finish, at your own pace, move your fingers, your feet, your hands and your shoulders. Now open your eyes, slowly stand up and stretch.*

After this exercise, you may feel a diffused or localized warmth, a slight dizziness, a tingling sensation in the extremities or even drowsiness. Don't worry! It's due to the increase of oxygen in your blood. If your body is not used to it, it may react with these kinds of symptoms. To avoid this, start with the amount of breathing suggested and gradually increase it. In the beginning, breathe as you normally would, through your nose or mouth. Little by little you will develop a habit of breathing in through your nose and out through your mouth. Focus on the sound of your exhaling. After a few sessions, you will be breathing through your nose for the entire exercise. Try breathing this way every day or as often as possible and observe the results.

3. NLP Visualization

Before starting, decide upon the desired state you wish to reach using visualization: calm, focus, confidence, peacefulness and so on. Start with a state that you want to reach but find relatively easy to achieve. Remember, small steps, mini-habits and patience!

Also decide what anchor point you will use. For example, snapping your fingers. It should be a discreet, specific gesture, rarely done at random.

Let's say that you choose: 'mental clarity' as your desired state.

- *Sit down in a comfortable place, close your eyes and concentrate on the sound of your breathing.*

Recall a situation - something rather recent - where your thoughts were really clear, your reasoning very lucid and your actions consistent with your ideas. Once you have thought of the situation, choose a precise moment, a bit like a freeze frame that, to you, represents the clarity and the lucidity of the whole situation.

- *Notice and observe all there is to see... people (if any), the place, objects... How is the image? Is it in color or black and white, blurry or clear, dark or bright? Is it moving or static, square or panoramic, are you in the frame? Remember everything that is visible in this moment of mental clarity.*

- *Next, listen to everything that you hear... the sounds, the voices... How is the sound? Is the volume strong or weak? Is the rhythm slow or fast? Is it close or far away? Is the tone high or low pitched? Is the sound inside of you or around you?*

- *Feel everything that there is to feel, take the time to let it spread throughout your body... Now, welcome the feeling of mental clarity that you had at this moment.*

- *In which part of the body do you feel it? What do you feel? Are you hot or cold, light or heavy, dry or humid? Is it smooth or rough? Is it inside of you or around you? Continue to see everything there is to see, to hear to*

81

everything there is to hear, to feel everything there is to feel. Continue to let it spread throughout you until you feel a strong mental clarity.

- *As soon as you see, hear and feel that your mental clarity is at its maximum, anchor it with a gesture of your choosing, such as rubbing your thumb and index finger together. Savor this mental clarity for a few moments.*

- *Repeat the anchoring, concentrate on your breathing - take your time. When you are ready, open your eyes, move your hands and feet and get up slowly.*

Conclusion

How the brain functions is very complex, but so interesting to explore! With these quick, simple Brain Gym® exercises you can reconnect your two hemispheres and optimize your effectiveness. Furthermore, the visualization and anchoring of positive feelings will help you to improve your performance and achieve your goals far more easily. Remember to practice abdominal breathing, both expansive and deep. This technique will help to calm down and refocus your mind faster.

Recharge your Emotional Batteries

Why?

Facts and ideas to explore your emotional energy

"What I don't own - owns me"

– Anonymous

In a nutshell, this quote summarizes the true value of managing our emotions. If we reject, ignore, or become a victim of them, they *own* us and we lose both their information and their power to motivate us.

When we experience an emotion, we become closer to what makes us feel human, both instinctively and intellectually. The Greek philosopher, Heraclitus, described life's eternal movement and impermanence as *panta rei*, meaning everything flows. Our emotions are a reflection of reality, full of nuances, constantly moving and though difficult to describe using intellect, they hugely impact all our choices and behaviors. They may motivate us immensely, overwhelm us or even block us. How do we express them? What is the interest in naming them more precisely and learning to identify them faster?

To help you with this, imagine a day without emotions. It would be almost impossible to choose, to feel pleasure or to express an opinion. But when we don't control them, our emotions are like a rudderless ship that leads us often to an unsatisfactory destination. However, when we listen to their message, they tell us if we feel at ease with what is happening and in which direction to head to find the satisfactions we wish.

Behavioral Model
Internal states are strongly connected
with our Emotional Energy

Therefore, we can say that when speaking of our emotions, we are also speaking of our well-being and of our needs. Fundamental needs such as hunger, thirst or fatigue are easily identified. But others are more ambiguous, like the need for recognition, sharing, belonging, closure, harmony or fairness.

Sometimes it is difficult to clearly express our emotions without mixing them up with our needs. In the 1960s, psychologist, Abraham Maslow, developed the *Hierarchy of Needs* concept. The most basic needs, connected to our survival, are found at the base of the pyramid, while those associated with our personal development are found at the top.

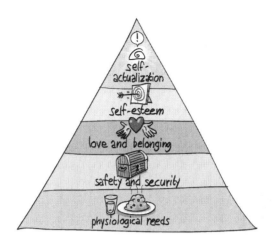

There is a logical hierarchy between the different levels: those at the bottom of the pyramid must be satisfied before we are fully able to focus on the ones higher up. Here is an example of what this means in your everyday life. Imagine that you get upset because your train is late, but what is the root of this emotion? Maybe you are just hungry or did not sleep well. Then again it could be a need for security, because you legitimately feel you should be able to rely on a regular schedule to get to work each morning. It could even be a need for fairness, as you've paid for your train pass and you expect reliable service in exchange. If you could identify the need at the root of your emotion, it would be easier for you to satisfy it and communicate what is happening to you. This would make yourself understood while respecting yourself and others around you. *Every emotion is only a manifestation of a deeper need.*

"Seek first to understand, and then be understood,"
– Stephen Covey

Observe the strategy that you choose to satisfy your needs. Are they healthy and sustainable? Are they clear to understand by the people around you? Do they support the quality of your life? Are they conducive to reaching your goals? How do they impact others?

Think of a time when you were angry and try and remember what it was you *really* wanted to express. For example, your child returned home much later than expected and, upon his return, you got angry. Indeed, your child disobeyed you and it is realistic to be upset. Yet, deep down inside, what *really* made you mad? Were you scared that something terrible could have happened? Or were your nerves just worn out? What is the need that triggered the anger? Is it a need to be heard? Is it a need for harmony?

Learning to separate the physical (and verbal) manifestations of the emotion from the underlying need that is causing it help us manage emotions much more easily - both ours and the emotions of others. Marshall B. Rosenberg developed a six-step process called *Non Violent Communication*, which offers a clear model to implement this idea. In his opinion, conflicts are never about our needs, they are about the strategies we put in place to satisfy our needs (shouting, procrastinating, spending too much, overworking and so on).

- *Observe* and describe the situation - the facts

- *Express* your emotions and thoughts connected to the facts and attitudes

- *Clarify* your underlying needs

- *Formulate* one clear question for the other party

- *Listen, with your full attention, to the answer*

- *Repeat what you have heard and come up with one clear behavior or action that would help you*

Usually, this process is repeated at least 2-3 times before reaching an agreement. Above all, keep listening!

Here is a list of needs and emotions from M. B. Rosenberg's book: Non-Violent Communication: a Language of Life (see Bibliography).

Needs	Emotions
autonomy	peacefulness
celebration	serenity
integrity	wonder
love	tenseness
respect	agitated
trust	confused
harmony	touched
rest	curious

Be patient: Everyone does what he or she can with what they have at any given time, you included.

The more you learn about what happens inside you, the more freedom you'll have to control your emotions and increase control over your actions on the outside. We can choose to feel annoyed or to deal with a problem calmly, but the decisions we make become conscious ones and are our responsibility. We will no longer be carried away by our emotions as often, or as easily.

Accessing our emotional resources also means releasing the energy blocked by anxiety of future events, anger, sadness about past situations, worries about the present. It important to note that no emotion is negative in itself! Once you identify an emotion, you uncover your need, choose how to respond and act with a stronger inner balance and a clearer mind.

The concept of emotional intelligence, popularized in the 1990s by Daniel Goleman, has clearly linked being in touch with our emotions with higher performance at work. Our communication becomes a more accurate reflection of how we feel, we are better understood, we better understand others. What's more, all these behaviors translate into an increased effectiveness.

In this book we will only focus on improving the communication with your *self*. If you wish to develop this approach for your communications with others or for your professional presentations, Dorotea Brandin has created an excellent method (see Bibliography).

Our Inner Dialogue

We give meaning to the events and communicate with ourselves through perceptions developed in our intellect, but  maintained by our inner dialogue. This is called the analysis-response loop, which occurs in three phases:

I perceive an event - through 3 main filters

I analyze it - through 3 main aspects

I respond - through 3 main types of responses

Of course, this loop is completed in less than a second! Moreover, we don't think about the path taken from feeling to attributing meaning to expressing. It's actually an automatic mechanism and we will now see a model which explains how we process information, before acting.

We have three categories of perception filters that together influence the way we interpret reality:

1. *Natural filters are our physiological limitations, like wearing glasses, being a man or a woman, having a less-developed sense of smell than a dog, and so on.*

2. *Socio-cultural filters are our views of the world in terms of our educational background, country of origin, the political climate and so on. A culture change causes us to challenge our filters.*

3. *Personal filters are based on our experiences, health, specific preferences, professional experience, etc.*

These three filters are useful to navigate and make sense of everyday experiences but might also act as barriers to produce:

Generalizations: It's always the same... I'm never lucky... That's the way it goes...

Distortions: Since you don't speak to me, you must not like me very much... I know what you're going to say...

Selections: This is the best... (For whom? In which sense?) That could happen... This is very important... (Why? According to which criteria?)

The information processed by our perception filters then goes through three analysis filters:

1. *The map of the world. All of our experiences stored in our memory make us navigate our way through life as if using a map. The map of the world is how we give meaning to events and create patterns and consistency from the various facts of our lives.*

2. *The structure of language. The choice of words we use every day to describe our experiences. They reinforce our emotions and beliefs. The alphabet is used, along with the direction of writing.*

3. *The structure of thought. The logic and organization of thoughts.*

Here are a few examples:

- The frame of reference: to refer to oneself or another before acting or thinking.

- The importance of content: to favor certain actions, people, places or things.

- Framing or zooming: specific (with a lot of detail) or global (an overview).

- The sensory filter: visual, auditory or kinesthetic.

- The sorting of information by its presence or absence: notice and retain what is present or what is missing, daily or in general.

Once we have gone through the filters of perception and analysis, there are three kinds of responses that we can choose from:

1. *Physical response: a movement of surprise, gestures, postures, a glance and so on. This is what is noticed first!*

2. *Verbal response: the choice of words, how we express what we have just analyzed.*

3. *Paraverbal response: the tone, musicality, rhythm and volume of the voice.*

For our response to be clear and powerful, these three kinds of responses must be consistent with one another. In fact, every day we see body movements that contradict associated words, like when someone physically recoils but says: "Oh, hello. I am delighted to see you!" Our bodies are almost *more revealing* than our words.

The more coherent and aligned these three responses are, the higher the chances that we are perceived as authentic and trustworthy. Remember that because of all the filters we use in our behavioral loop, we tell ourselves stories or create scenarios in which we believe. Sometimes, especially if we are not aware of our filters, they can put us into all sorts of states. Let's put this into a realistic situation.

An event occurs: I have a meeting with my boss and she asks me to meet her privately in her office. I analyze: I scan my various filters to choose how to respond. Is she upset, does she want to ask me to finish my report? Last time she asked me to go to her office was to complain about my presentation. She looks relaxed, though. I also relax.

I choose my behavior: I smile and ask if 2pm would be fine. This short interaction requires our brain to focus and choose between a huge amount of data, of potential meanings and possible responses.

In addition to the analysis-response loop, our brain doesn't know the difference between real and imagined events and produces strong chemicals activities in both cases.

Researches show that looking at peaceful images (landscapes, babies, pets and so on) triggers the production of serotonin - a hormone which contributes to a sense of well-being, while looking at violent images (war, cruel or violent behavior), triggers cortisol and adrenaline.

Let's explore how to use words to foster more empowering emotions.

The Code-Name System

To structure our reality, in a way that helps not hinders us, we can give the experience a code-name, a sort of label that will enable us to distance ourselves from what we label as a problem in order to see it in another light and find a solution faster.

Here is a very simple exercise to help you better understand the code-name system:

- *Think about a beautiful place, a place that you find uplifting and nurturing, where you feel safe and protected. It might be a real place or an imaginary one.*

   Look at it more closely, listen to all the sounds, and take in the feelings. Explore what you see, hear and feel in this place.

   When you have it fully in front of you, record all of its enjoyable features. Assign a code-name that encompasses the place's characteristics, such as "light", "orange", or "pleasure". Choose what feels appropriate to you. If you chose the word "orange", you will notice that this word now triggers the positive feelings that you felt in your special place.

You can also train yourself to distance yourself from emotions that are draining your energy and upsetting your inner balance. Begin with small events that may annoy you, like the long line at the supermarket checkout, the bus being late again and so on. We reinforce or change our beliefs and emotions according to the label we attach to events.

- *Remember an unpleasant time, visualize it, think of its colors, listen to the sounds, feel everything there is to feel and then give it a code-name representative of all these characteristics. It can be "grey", "foggy," or "pressure".*

  If the code-name chosen is "grey", you'll notice that this word on its own represents that moment.

  Now use the abdominal breathing technique to both visualize and feel that this "grey" goes outside of you.

  Start with a mildly upsetting event that you want to feel more peaceful about. Once you are more at ease with this technique, choose events that affected you more. This technique is effective for every day disagreements, but not for seriously traumatic events.

Your inner dialogue, as it rarely stops, guides your emotions and influences your actions. However, you are fully able to direct it and, therefore, focus your energy on the emotions that motivate and strengthen you. If your inner dialogue follows a formula like "*reassure, encourage and congratulate*", you are your best ally. You will have a clear understanding of your needs and your vulnerabilities, and you will accept them as they are, with fewer judgments and criticisms.

Do you know the programs on your mental radio? Or you spend more time listening to the "*Anxiety and Doubt Show*"? If so, try to change the station tune into the "*Lightness and Confidence*" frequency, and watch what happens in your daily life. If it seems too difficult at first, start by changing the program for just a few minutes.

As I have already said, everyone does what he or she can with what they have at any given time. It's not a matter of minimizing a problem, a concern or a depressing moment. It is more a matter of being both kind and honest, while observing how your inner dialogue is reproducing the same patterns and beliefs that are causing your struggles. When you learn to modify your inner dialogue's program, the new choice of words might seem strange or forced. This is true and also part of the learning process. Accept this idea for now and try it out for one week. Then, observe whether the perception of you and of the events associated with you have changed and decide if it is worth continuing with the experiment. Internal dialogue can be discouraging without you even being aware. Therefore, it might help if you jot down a few observations every day.

When you try out these exercises, should your predominant disposition be to notice what's lacking or what you want to avoid, then you risk telling yourself that this change in your internal dialogue isn't working. However, if you are aware of this preference, it is already easier to address it and notice when it is useful and when it is sabotaging your efforts.

In NLP jargon, this preference to notice what you want to avoid is referred to as a *Meta Program* and is called *Away from*. There is no value judgment in this term, as you have with the terms pessimist or perfectionist. You might find it useful to identify your own *Meta Programs* and explore how these preferences affect your choices, your perceptions and your emotions.

A *Meta Program* is defined as a pattern that helps us to process and make sense of the information, facts and situations that we face. The strength of our preference to use this particular *Meta Program* might also depend on the context, along with our individual history and current mindset. Like other models we have explored, the interest here is to become more aware of your patterns and how they affect your quality of life. This will allow you to control where it makes sense to direct your energy.

On the next page you find a list of the *Meta Programs* from Mo Shapiro's excellent book: *Neuro-Linguistic Programming*. This extremely useful book was written for managers who wish to use NLP in their work, though it is relevant for any professional. See the Bibliography at the end for further references.

The language column briefly describes the words most often associated with the *Meta Programs* and the final column suggests additional words you might use to establish rapport. (see table on next page)

META PROGRAMS	language they use	work pattern / role	your response
towards	get, have, gain attain, accomplish	sales, innovation, inventor, designer	goal oriented, hope for, incentives
away from	avoid, steer clear, exclude, prevent	problem solving, health & safety	point out dangers of not doing, exclude
match	usual, familiar, in common	mediation, trends, negotiation	same as, traditional
mismatch	new, change, on-off, different	marketing, consultancy	unique, special, revolutionary
internal reference	I decide, I made the decision...	web design, writer, performer, lawyer	only you can decide, only you will know
external reference	what do you think? Is that OK?	PA., bank teller, travel agent, civil servant	others think, the facts show
general	overall big picture, globally flexible	explorer, policy maker, strategy	basically, framework, overview, roughly
detail	specifically, precisely, schedule	pilot, architect, finance, editor	structure, exactly, let's be clear
options	choice, possibility	teachers	alternatives, options
procedure	needed to, must	filing accounts	known, way, proven
proactive	initiative, action, future plans	fundraiser, journalist, sales, entrepreneur	independent, direct
reactive	respond, reaction, past achievement	help desk, call center, receptionist	analysis, waiting

Benefits of closed and open words

As with our internal dialogue, when we verbalize a description of events it influences our emotions, just as much as the facts. Our choice of words can make us motivated players in our lives or unhappy spectators.

Closed words are about obstacles, struggles, what is not going as we wish. They focus on problems and are likely to wake up your 'limbic brain', triggering fight, fly or freeze reactions.

Open words are about choices, free will, and development of our potential. They focus on solutions and opportunities and are likely to wake up your neocortex, the area of your brain responsible for creative and thinking out-of-the-box.

How?
Tools and techniques to try out

To put into practice the ideas we just explored, here four extremely useful techniques.

They are likely to take longer than the techniques in the previous chapters, since they touch your emotions and beliefs more directly.

1. *Language Booster*

2. *Observe - Acknowledge - Accept*

3. *Step-By-Step Visualization*

4. *Inner Dialogue*

1. Language Booster

Observe and recognize the words that judge and criticize your *self*, other people or events. If you use them often, you might feel discouraged. You will find that it's possible to avoid them and find a different way to express them. Below I have provided a series of closed, limiting words and expressions, with questions you can use to challenge them.

List of closed words:

"I must, I should, I shouldn't have…"
You deny your *self* the power to choose and you assume the role of *victime du devoir*, meaning victim of duty.

Also it polarizes the situation into right or wrong, yes or no, and potentially misses out new options. *Question: Who said that you must/that you should have?* Do you still agree with this?

"It is necessary, it should be necessary… "
Where is your freedom?
Question: Why it is necessary? What could happen if you act differently?

"Always, never, anyway, all… "
When these words are followed by a negative opinion about your qualities.
Question: Always, really? Every time, really? Which situations are different?

"It's not normal… "
Does your idea of normality help or hinder you?
Question: What is normal? And who defines it?
Which are the values supported by that this definition of 'normality'? Do you agree with them?

"The problem is… "
You are looking for a solution, an opportunity or a challenge, labeling a situation as a 'problem' which reinforces the negative impact it has on you.
Question: What are the facts? What opportunities does this situation offer?

"I will try to… "

Using 'try' dilutes the power of your intentions. You might say, "I will see what I can do", which already changes the outlook. *Suggestion: Place an object in front of you and "try to take it". Did you take it?*

"It's a disaster, horrible, dead, I hate it. It is disgusting"

And all the negative superlatives describing everyday events (missed train, jammed printer or spilled coffee.) *Question: Is it really a disaster? To start with, choose a less dramatic word: annoying, upsetting, inconvenient.*

"I am tired to death, exhausted, a wreck… "

And all these expressions that exaggerate an unpleasant state or describe the situation as permanent. It's an excellent way to self-condition, but negatively. *Suggestion: I could be in better shape, I am slowly feeling better, I am sure that I will…*

Any sentence that conveys a sense of dynamic evolution and flow is better.

We also create what is known as a distortion by using phrases that make external events or others responsible for our emotions.

"I'm upset because she… I can't do it because of the deadline… I have no choice since they… "

Suggestion: It's not the other person who upsets you, but

their behavior that triggers an emotion in you. Ask yourself, where does this emotion come from? Which are the needs or values that you feel are not met as you wished?

"He doesn't really appreciate me and never pays me any compliments… "

Question: Who said that all bosses must pay explicit compliments? Does he show his appreciation of your work in other ways?

List of open words

The list of open words is more personal and far more diversified than the list of closed words. You can create a list for yourself and put it as a reminder on your computer or save them in your cell phone.

"I can, I could… "

"I am free to…"

"I decided to, I want… "

"I trust myself to…"

"I'm becoming more and more… I'm improving… I'm learning to…"

In fact, all verbs that express movement towards a goal will help you.

"I am able to...I am more able to…"

"I am grateful that... fortunate that... I seized my chance..."

Any phrases that recognize an enjoyable event or a positive development will help.

"There's a chance... the goal / the solution / the challenge is..."

Any words that describe opportunities and not problems will help this process.

2. Observe - Acknowledge - Accept

- *It's not always easy to feel at peace, whether it's about the past, present or the future - even if intellectually we know that it would be better for us and for those around us. There are three main steps that are useful to follow before you decide what to do: observe, acknowledge and accept. If you follow these steps, you will be more aligned with your goals and values when you act, since you have collected both the facts and the emotions linked to the situation. This process is based primarily on the*

observation of facts. Observe your behaviors attentively, make note of the details and give labels to your emotions. If possible, identify the needs underneath the emotions. You have given both hemispheres a chance to respond. The right brain for the big picture and the left brain for the language and the details.

For example, if you had decided to dedicate 10 minutes each day to yourself, but two days have now passed without doing anything you should do the following:

Observe the facts, but do not overwhelm yourself with criticism, such as "*I'm no good, I never keep my commitments, my resolutions are useless*". Instead, name the facts What is happening exactly? Gather data so you will know what is working and what needs to be tweaked or adapted.

Acknowledge your emotions, such as the feeling of failure (I never kept my promise), impatience (I have to get it done) or lack of confidence (I'm no good). From there, ask yourself what you can change the next time in order to achieve a different result involving different emotions.

Accept your emotions and the fact that you need to change something. Now identify what - in your present situation - you can control, what you can influence and what you need to accept for the time being. Then decide if you need to tweak your new habit to a quicker, smaller, or simpler one to make it more effective and easier to implement. For example, simply try 5 minutes instead of 10.

Sometimes your emotions are just too strong to apply this process and the following visualization will help you reduce the intensity that you experience related to a specific topic (a person, situation, or an event).

3. Step-By-Step Visualization

Here are some general guidelines for when you carry out a visualization exercise of this kind:

- *Ensure that you are comfortable during the exercise. You can adjust your posture, your muscles, tone, your chair or even your clothing. You can also create a comfortable anchor, such as wearing the same t-shirt for these exercises.*

  Repeat the visualization as many times as you want, but always evaluate the emotional intensity at the beginning and at the end of the exercise to better observe the results. Use a scale of 1-10 (1 being a very low intensity and 10 for very high). You will quickly see your progress.

Sit in a comfortable position and close your eyes. Think of an unpleasant situation from the past (but not traumatic) that still bothers you, despite your best efforts to turn over a new page. Evaluate the actual emotional impact on a scale from 1-10.

- *With your eyes closed, imagine that you are sitting in a chair at the cinema, in front of a large white screen. You are alone and you are holding a remote control in your right hand.*

  On the screen, look at this situation and remember the specific moment, where you were, the time and who was present.

  Explore those details on the screen. Look at the colors, the movements, the size of the people, their distance in relation to yourself and so on.

  Watch, listen, and experience everything there is to see, hear, and feel.

  Now, touch your forehead with your fingers and find a comfortable position to keep them in until the end of the visualization.

  Return to your situation and, while watching the screen, listen again to the noises and voices that were there.

  Breakdown the sounds associated with this situation: their volume, rhythm, origin (from the front, behind, beside the screen).

Again, watch, listen, and experience everything there is to see, hear, and feel.

With the pictures and sounds, try to feel everything that you find in this situation. Determine where your feelings are coming from within your body - their consistency, colors and movements.

Now, with your remote control, fiddle with the picture. Scramble it, dull the colors. If you are still in the picture, see yourself leaving it.

Change the audio controls. Lower the volume, scramble the rhythm, and make the sounds go far away.

Change the kinesthetic controls. If you are cold, wrap yourself with a blanket; if it is hot, imagine a wave of fresh air.

Using your remote control, associate your feelings to the pictures and sounds on the screen and reduce their intensity.

Now, look, listen and feel what's left of the situation on the screen.

Reduce then move the size of the image and decrease the volume, make a ball out of what is left, then reduce the size of the ball and get ready to throw it away!

From here, you can get rid of it either with your remote control or by moving your arm like when you throw a real ball. Count: 1, 2, 3 go!

Watch it disappear into the distance. Breathe in and out a couple of times and start to come back to the present.

At your own pace, move your hands, feet and shoulders. Think about the situation again and re-evaluate its emotional impact on you, still on a scale from 1-10.

See if there is a difference. When you are ready, open your eyes and get up slowly to stretch.

Once you have become familiar with the process, you can simplify it and use it to calm yourself after a conflict or a difficult interview. There are multiple applications.

4. Inner Dialogue

- *Find time during the day when you can be alone for 15 minutes. Get a sheet of paper and a pen. Think about the way you speak about yourself and about the person with*

113

whom you are talking. Do you belittle yourself with your sentences? Do you make generalizations (I'll never be able to...) or comparisons – either by measuring against others or with an ideal, making it very difficult to obtain an image of yourself (I should, I must)?

Write down all of these recurring sentences, especially those that you repeat on a daily basis and that express a negative opinion about your skills or your personality. Also, write down the sentences that you might use in a humorous way but have an underlining criticism. Look at the sentences that you've written. You will find that they are often static and fixed in time. Now, transform them into more encouraging ones which will be more dynamic and open to change. Here are a few examples:

"I will never be able to... "
(...drive well, keep calm when people scream, be patient)
This might become: *"I am learning to... "*

"I'm always... "
(...late with deadlines, messy, easily angered)
You may question this with: *"When? And in which context? Is it always true? In which situations do I not behave in this way?"*

"I'm terrible at..."
(...filling spread sheets, presentations, answering my

emails) These questions may become: *"All the time? Has it changed through the years?" Who could help me? What is this statement based on?"*

Listen To Your Words

- *Observe your personal language for a few days (three or four are enough) and make a list of your most common expressions. Notice if*  *they are open or closed and then choose at least two expressions to reformulate. Use the reformulations for a week and observe the results. You are likely to feel more at peace with yourself and more in control of your emotions when a situation is not going the way you want.*

You have now taken one more step in the analysis of the creative power of your language. Observe yourself, maintain your flexibility and your sense of humor.

Above all, be patient. Reassure yourself, encourage yourself and congratulate yourself.

Conclusion

The more accurately you can identify your emotions, the easier it is to learn from them and move on without carrying the burden of unresolved issues or recurring self-defeating behaviors. Think about distinguishing your emotions from your needs, and your strategies. Encourage yourself to go from using closed words (problem oriented) to open words (solution oriented). When you are in touch with your emotions and they *synergize* with your thoughts, your are able to understand yourself and others more readily and others will also understand you much faster.

Recharge your
Spiritual Batteries

Why?
Facts and ideas to explore your spiritual energy

Victor Frankle, author of *Man's search for Meaning*, wrote that if we can find the *why*, we can live with *any* how. His shattering experiences in Nazi concentration camps gave him the need to find meaning to the events. Why was this happening? Why did I want to keep on living? He also needed to understand its impact on the survival of his comrades. Those without hope or a plan to imagine living beyond the end of the war died more quickly than those who created future goals, enabling them to overcome the horrors they endured every day.

After our basic physiological needs are met (e.g. water, sleep, food and shelter), our values and beliefs are the most powerful source of our energy.

We all endure, refuse or overcome situations that seemed impossible to solve or support a cause, a vision or other beings in need. Spiritual energy might include the transcendent. However, in this book, it refers to personal values and to the purpose we give to our life and to the world. Values and beliefs are often used interchangeably. In our exploration of spiritual resources, we will differentiate them.

Values are the moral principles from what we consider events and behaviors, such as good or bad, positive or negative, useful or useless, important or trivial - they are all very personal. When someone criticizes something we say or do, it might be unsettling because the subject of his or her criticism touches and upsets a dear value. For example, your colleague says, "*It's ridiculous to take notes by hand nowadays. That's what computers are for!*" You will either be annoyed or in complete agreement with him depending on whether you share the value advanced by the criticism or not (in this case it might be 'sincerity'). Values are also our reservoir of self-motivation.

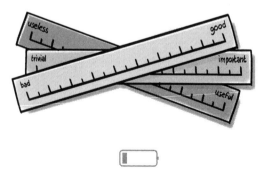

Beliefs are the opinions we choose (consciously or not) which provide insight into how we give meaning to our reality (what we think about money, health, success, the army and so on). In Chapter 3 on emotional resources, we explored emotions and needs. Our beliefs often affect our needs and emotions, hence the interest to be fully aware of them. Here are three very general examples that you can apply to many situations.

"I'll never be able to..." This may indicate a belief that some types of knowledge are beyond your comprehension or that you don't have the necessary resources to overcome your challenges.

"I need more..." This may refer to a belief about prosperity and abundance.

"You have to work hard for a good life..." This might indicate a lack of self-confidence: "I don't know how to manage my money."

You are the only person that knows the underlying belief in the expressions that you use the most often, or the thoughts that cross your mind many times each day. If you wish to explore your beliefs, following is one to way to do it.

Start a sentence like this: "I believe that... health is..." and end it as you like, as often as needed.

These are some areas where you could check your current beliefs: health, money, relationship, work, happiness, success, failures, growing old, conflict, your body, material possessions, people and family.

Start with the ones that feel most important to you.

When you find a belief that expresses a fearful or negative opinion, you might ask yourself where it comes from.

Some beliefs may stem from your childhood or from what your parents or teachers said many years ago. Very often they were told with good intentions, but poorly formulated, producing a feeling of scarcity, lack or danger. *"You're better than that... Let the adults talk... You have nothing interesting to say..."*

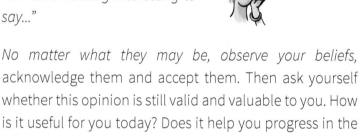

No matter what they may be, observe your beliefs, acknowledge them and accept them. Then ask yourself whether this opinion is still valid and valuable to you. How is it useful for you today? Does it help you progress in the direction closest to your heart or does it take you away from it?

Does it support your current goals? Take the time you need to reflect and explore.

Based on these reflections, update your beliefs and keep only those that support and empower you. It might be a good idea to go through your beliefs every few years. The objective is to increase awareness of yourself and to improve the quality of your life at all levels. By updating your values and beliefs you will continue to grow and transform your current limitations into valuable resources.

* *Let's now examine values. From the following list, choose five values that are instinctively the most important to you - if a value is not on the list, simply add it.*

Values	
spirituality	recognition
sharing	love
severity	harmony
solidarity	truth
loyalty	integrity
authenticity	sincerity
generosity	fairness
freedom	brotherhood

Make a note of them and allow 4-5 days to pass. Then, look at your list again and see if it is still valid or if you want to change something.

Now, read again what you wrote about your beliefs in the most important areas of your life: health, family, prosperity, work, success, happiness, friendship, etc.

Then compare this list with the one containing your values and ask yourself: "Are my beliefs and my values aligned? Are they different and in conflict with one another? If I answered yes, what can I do to find harmony? Which one do I want to change? Which ones can I let go?"

We have seen many times the Behavioral Model of interdependence between our thoughts, emotions and physical responses. Using the same model, values are represented (as well as beliefs) by a second circle that includes the first one and forms the frame of reference for our choices. The consistency and alignment between these four levels increase the quality of our life on each level.

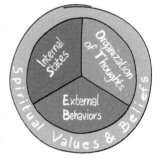

Awareness of our values strengthens our ability to rebound from the unexpected as well as our ability to enjoy reality.

Benefits of gratitude

> "We have what we recognize we have,"
> – *G. Jampolsky*

As Gerald Jampolsky wrote, we have only what we recognize we have. This recognition isn't just intellectual; it must be accompanied by a feeling of abundance that reassures us and gives us an inner peace that we have everything we need.

But we are very often stuck in the fast pace of our lives and we focus our attention more on what we lack, still wish for or want to change. How many times have we made our serenity conditional upon an object, an event or a person?

And when we get what we want, like a new outfit, a better job, or a partner, the cycle starts over again. We can choose to live in abundance or in focus of our unfulfilled desires.

The word gratitude comes from the Latin word *gratia*, which means good will, esteem or regard. I would like to take this etymology one step further and connect it with what I regard as being favorable, depending on my goodwill to see it this way. Gratitude then becomes a synonym of recognition. If you express your gratitude for what you already have, it enables you to *know it again* - to recognize it - appreciate it and make it flourish more. Learn how to create a quiet space in which to unwind and recharge yourself, even If you are in the middle of a busy place.

How?

Tools and techniques to try out

These four techniques take longer than the ones described until now since they explore your values and beliefs. However they equally increase and balance all the other levels of your energy. Make sure that you have the time and the space to experience them peacefully.

The four techniques are:

1. Gratitude List

2. Your Energy Budget

3. Silent Sitting

4. The Mirror Tree

1. Gratitude List

* *To start this exercise, find a quiet time in which you can be alone for about 10 minutes.*

  Use a sheet of paper and a pen and copy the list below, leaving a 5 cm space between the words.

couple	friendship	health
finances	professional life	family
housing	beliefs & values	environment

127

Next, underneath each of these words, write what is currently contributing to your well-being.

Note the details as much as the elements that seem important to you. For example, under 'housing' you might note things such as cactus in bloom, renovated bathroom or reasonable rent, etc.

Complete this list, put the sheet of paper somewhere visible for at least three days and observe the impact it has on your perceptions and how you feel.

Even if you want to make changes in some areas, starting from a place of gratitude and mental abundance, it gives you a more sustainable energy than starting from a place of criticism and mental scarcity.

2. Your Energy Budget

What is your available energy? Here is an exercise that will provide you with an overview of what recharges you and what drains your energy.

Find a time during the day when you can be alone for around 15 minutes. Have two sheets of paper and a pen.

- *Sit comfortably and take a few abdominal breaths, focusing on breathing out a bit slower and a bit longer than you usually do.*

On one sheet of paper, write down what recharges you: activities (work, running, reading), people (friends, children), alone time, thoughts (memories, hopes, projects), habits (listening to music, taking a shower in the morning, keeping a journal) or other categories.

On the other sheet of paper, write down what saps or drains your energy. If it helps you, you can divide these rechargers and drainers into four levels: physical, mental, emotional and spiritual.

Re-read what you have written and isolate the recurring themes. For example: being with people you know well relaxes you; learning new things stimulates you; continuous interruptions in your work disturb you, and so on.

Compare the two lists and observe yourself for a week to collect more information. Examine the lists again. What patterns do you notice?

What can you learn? What could you do more? What could you do less? What could you stop?

3. Silent Sitting

The goal of this technique is to reconnect you with your inner strength in order to calm your mind. To fully benefit from it, use it for at least ten days. You'll only need about three minutes a day, a few times a week. It is inspired by *Tonglen*, which is a more complex form of meditation in Tibetan Buddhism, based on compassion and opening the heart to others' suffering.

It is normal that all kinds of thoughts come up during this exercise. When that happens, bring your focus either to the person who inspires you to love and be compassionate, or to the person to whom you are sending love. Find a time during the day when you can be alone for 5-6 minutes.

• *Sit comfortably and take a few abdominal breaths, breathing out a bit longer and slower than usual.*

Keep your eyes open and look at the ground about a meter in front of you. Focus on the sound of your breathing.

Think of a cherished person or an animal that awakens love and compassion within you. Visualize them coming

to greet you. See what you need to see and hear what you need to hear. Feel what there is to feel. For example, it might feel like a gentle warmth embraces you. Let this warmth soothe your wounds and ease your disappointments. Think of a sad feeling that you wish to let go and immerse it into this warmth.

After a moment, imagine that this cherished person or animal turns into a soft light. See this soft light inside your body (maybe in the heart, the stomach... choose your place) and let it stay there, always ready for you to access and use its healing warmth.

When you feel ready, send your love to other people or animals around you.

Conclude by focusing on the soft light and surrounding yourself with love and compassion.

When you are ready, reconnect to your breathing. Slowly move your hands, feet, shoulders and your neck. Then get up slowly and stretch.

4. The Mirror Tree

Different from other techniques, this last technique is designed for occasional practice and therefore lasts longer. Find a time during the day where you can be alone for at least 20 minutes. If music helps you to relax and to focus, put it on.

- *Use colored pencils or markers and sheets of paper, the size and color you want.*

  Sit comfortably and take 3-4 abdominal breaths to get comfortable in the present moment, in the here and now.

  Think of yourself as a tree with its roots and begin to draw what comes, using pictures, words or symbols to create your tree.

  Identify and acknowledge your roots. Where do they come from? From your culture, your family, your love of nature, or your friends? Add any details you wish.

  Now, imagine the trunk and the branches. What is essential in order for your mental and emotional health to grow? What is important for your relationships or to motivate you?

  Look at your branches. How do you reach out to what matters to you? How do you connect and interact with

the world? It's here where your growth is embodied and finds its shape and direction.

To conclude, draw flowers and fruits. How do you want to contribute to the world? What do you wish to give, say or share? This is where your vision of the world will materialize.

To finish, look at the tree in its entirety. What is the general impression you get? Which parts feel more harmonious? Which ones feel more vulnerable and in need of energy? What might these parts represent in your life?

Put your drawing in a place where you can see it often and easily, allowing the answers to emerge over time. The answers sometimes take longer to emerge, particularly for this exercise. Be patient with your rhythm.

Observe, recognize and accept what this Mirror Tree shows you today.

Conclusion

The spiritual resources we have defined here - the beliefs and values that give meaning and guide us throughout our lives - are the roots of our very being, they nourish and sustain our physical, mental and emotional energy. Choose from this chapter, one new way to interpret the events, that would be both useful and easy to implement, remember the idea of small habits: too small to fail. In the beginning, your goal is to anchor a little change, not to radically reboot how you manage your spiritual energy! In my experience, the lasting changes are both imperceptible and fairly pleasing to implement.

Remember: observe, recognize, accept and be patient!

Conclusion

Conclusion

At this point in the book, you have explored the four components of your energy and now know how they influence your actions and your quality of life. You have also learned about new ideas to recharge your batteries. I hope that you found the content relevant and that you are now motivated to put some of these tools into action.

Your next step is to translate these theories and exercises into sustainable habits and integrate them into a personal self-care routine. Please remember that you can download a template for your routine from my website: www.pem.pm - which you can find easily in the section 'Try it out'.

As a coach, I know from experience that there are key points that turn a *good resolution* (like those we make at the beginning of a new year) into a *good habit,* requiring little or no willpower (like brushing your teeth). Here is what I suggest to give yourself all the chances to succeed with your new habits.

One thing at a time

Begin by putting into practice one technique only, two at the most. Many *good resolutions* are impossible to keep, as they need too much time. Trust the snowball effect - one success leads to another. This also means that your start small and only expand once your new habit or technique has roots.

A smooth start

Ask yourself which technique is the easiest to apply for you. Consider developing the habit before improving its quality.

This will come over time. Think about what you do with a child. You begin by teaching her to brush her teeth before going to bed and then you ensure her that she does it well. As humans, we like predictability and learning new things takes effort. Therefore, identify one of your points of least resistance and start from there to change.

An accurate roadmap

Put into writing, as accurately as possible, how you will use the techniques. Ask yourself, for example, what is your ultimate goal and what are the signs of your progress? To draw a clearer roadmap, ask yourself the following questions and write down the answers:

- *How many times per week will you use this technique?*

- *At what time of day?*

- *In which context, such as location, ambiance, etc.?*
- *How will you remember your decision?*
- *With whom can you share your good resolution?*
- *With whom can you occasionally check that you are making progress?*
- *How will you celebrate your accomplishments?*

The more specific you are about these questions the better your chances of reaching your goals.

A commitment of 80% of the time

The snowball effect I spoke about earlier will be felt if you keep your new resolutions and if you use these techniques at least 80% of the time. Of course, you must deal with unexpected situations that sometimes prevent you from acting as you have decided; this is life, it doesn't always go exactly as planned.

If you expect a 100% from yourself, you are likely to become demotivated by your own impossible high standards... and stop everything when you have a set back.

Celebrate each step

Think of a child learning to walk. He takes a few steps and falls, but we comfort him and encourage him to start over, "Bravo, very good!" The child gets up, tries again and falls once more and so we encourage him again. So goes the learning cycle, until the ability to walk is acquired. Now, imagine that you tell the child that he is unable to coordinate his movements, that his tiny steps are really pathetic and that his balance is unsatisfactory. If we behaved that way, I wonder how any people could have ever learned to walk.

Treat yourself as you would treat a beloved friend that you want to encourage and motivate. The path of sustainable balance goes through patience, clear goals and a lot of humor towards yourself and the events that mark your life. Each of us has a valuable freedom - the ability to choose how we respond to events.
Use this freedom to your advantage!

Please remember that the power of small steps and gentle perseverance will create a new and more sustainable dynamic to manage your energy, your performance and the quality of your life.

"Practice makes possible before it makes perfect"

Artie Egendorf

+

Bibliography

This bibliography reflects my choice of resources which will allow you to further explore the themes I describe in my book.

Due to the fact that resources can be easily found on the Internet, I have only listed minimal references for the books and added more videos and websites, apps, webinars, articles for quicker 'dip-ins' and a wider choice of means.

Please feel free to contact me for more specific references at: info@pem.pm

+

1. General about Personal Energy Management

I. Videos

Video of Tony Schwartz explaining the 4 energies.
There is also a short text that explains the 4 energies.
http://www.theenergyproject.com/tools/key-ideas/four-forgotten-needs

4-minute video of T.S. talking about establishing 'rituals' (habits).
www.theenergyproject.com/about/videos/develop-productivity-rituals

Very short video from T.S. about pulsing and wave-like energy management.
It highlights a good point about the need to renew after intense efforts or too little effort.
http://www.theenergyproject.com/tools/key-ideas/performance-zone

17-minute TED Talk video of Stanford professor BJ Fogg on mini habits (he calls them tiny habits). Some parts are not so clear but overall it is useful.
https://www.youtube.com/watch?v=AdKUJxjn-R8

II. Websites

Tony Schwartz website:
www.thenergyproject.com

Jim Loher website:
www.jjhpi.com

III. Books

Instant Calm, by Paul Wilson.
A very good and clear description of more than 100 techniques. No overall red thread on how to use the various tools but really useful if you look for ideas and short, clear explanations.

The Full Power Of Engagement, by Jim Loher and Tony Schwartz.
This book is still the main reference for 'energy management' in English.

Presence, by Amy Cuddy.
Here you can find many of the scientific researches that my book refers too and many other really interesting reflections on the nature of being truly 'present' so we are able 'bring your boldest self to your biggest challenges'. A great read.

✦

2. About Physical Energy

I. Videos

6-minute extract of a longer video linking physical activity and mental attitude. From Ellen Langer.
http://youtu.be/YVAhbcWk1KA?t=39m21s

6-minute video with Amy Cuddy from Harvard talking about body language and the influence on brain performances.
http://www.youtube.com/watch?v=zmR2A9TnIso

Sitting Kills, Moving Heals, by the NASA researcher, Dr. Joan Vernikos.
Her book is short, but well written and offers easy to implement suggestions.
http://www.youtube.com/watch?v=TKjr-az3xeE

II. Websites

On this website you will find a wide variety of free downloads for *yoga nidra*.
They are guided visualizations that aim at increasing the quality of your sleep.
It is important that you find a voice that is soothing, so keep on browsing until you find a voice that you connect with.
http://www.yoganidranetwork.org/downloads

✝

This is a really well-documented website relating to nutrition and interval training (20m are enough), by Dr. Jade Teta. It follows guidelines instead of rules with a focus on discovering what works best for each one.
www.metaboliceffect.com

III. Books

Counter Clock Wise Health, by E.Langer.
A fascinating book detailing edge studies linking physical health with expectations, mindsets and language choices. Also available as an audio book.

Instant Calm, by Paul Wilson.
A very good and clear description of more than 100 techniques.

The Metabolic Effect Diet, by Jade Teta.
A clear and effective approach to interval training and basics nutrition. He has an excellent website with online video courses.

+

3. About Mental Energy
I. Videos

15-minute video for leaders about the link between brain, and its effectiveness and why knowing about this connection will improve your ability to change your mental states.
By David Rock (see Books).
https://www.youtube.com/watch?v=uDIyxxayNig

27-minute video about how our brain has 2 distinct modes to process: fast and slow…and about the implications of these 2 different speeds.
Based on the book: Thinking fast-thinking slow, by Daniel Kahnemann.
https://www.youtube.com/watch?v=mWaIE6u3wvw

4-minute video on how to break a habit
From the website of Charles Duhigg: The Power of Habits.
Author of the very well-researched book with the same title.
http://charlesduhigg.com/how-to-break-habits/

II. Websites

The website of David Rock - Your brain at work - full of the latest researches on neurosciences and management.

http://www.davidrock.net/resources/index.shtml

The website of Paul Denison who created the Brain Gym®
www.braingym.org

III. Books

Focus, by Daniel Goleman
His latest book links focus, performances and mindfulness.
For practical exercises based on this book, please go to:
https://www.morethansound.net

Your Brain At Work, by David Rock.
You will find facts and information on 'neuroleadership'.
Very interesting if you wish to know what happens inside
the brain when we face various professional situations.

4. About Emotional Energy
I. Videos

5-minute video that shows how stress and anxiety affects
the different areas of the brain. Well done and very visual.
https://www.youtube.com/watch?v=gmwiJ6ghLIM

Short intro to emotional Intelligence
3.5-minute of good old EI at work. Nice basic, calm voice
from the lady presenter.
http://www.youtube.com/watch?v=PG3Ea7nzNsA

✛

II. Books

Living Non-Violent Communication, by Marshal Rosenberg.
A 4-step method to solve conflicts, listen with the heart and find alignment. Very effective and easy to try out.

Neuro Linguistic Programming, by Mo Shapiro.
Excellent book on how you can try out other NLP (neuro-linguistic programming) tools in a professional context (meetings, appraisals etc.)
On Amazon.co.uk

Speak With Your Audience, by Dorotea Brandin.
Great method to connect with your needs and express them with impact in a professional and personal context.
On Amazon.com

Your Brain at Work, by David Rock.
You will find facts and information on 'neuroleadership'. Very interesting if you wish to know what happens inside the brain when we face various professional situations.

5. About Spiritual Energy
I. Videos

A well done, easy-to-follow TED talk video by neuroscientist Sara Lazar, who shows how meditation can actually change the size of key regions of our brain, improving our

+

memory and making us more empathetic, compassionate, and resilient under stress.

The link will take you exactly to where she talks about brain and meditation.

http://youtu.be/m8rRzTtP7Tc?t=5m14s

II. Websites

If you like to browse for books, audio files, blogs and podcasts, this website offers a wide variety on mindfulness, leadership and emotional intelligence.

https://www.morethansound.net

If you wish to explore energy at all levels - especially the emotional and spiritual ones- try this body-based approach that will gently and effectively lead you into expanding your awareness: www.energysway.com

III. Books

Man's Search for Meaning, by Victor Frankle.

A moving reflection of how we give meaning to our lives and how this affects our motivation to live. Frankle survived time in a concentration camp.

✝

Jonathan Livingstone Seagull, by Richard Bach.
A very short book about a seagull that devotes its life to learn and perfect the art of flying.

The Alchemist, by Paulo Cohelo.
A book about the quest of a boy for his dreams. It's a short but poetic book.

Zen And The Art Of Motorcycle Maintenance, by Robert Pirsig.
A fiction book that blends Eastern and Western philosophies.

The three marriages, by David Whyte.
The author- a poet and previously a 'busy professional' himself, explores the integration of work, relationships and self, going beyond the 'work-life balance' approach. Refreshing and inspiring.

The heart aroused: poetry and the preservation of the soul in corporate America, by David Whyte.
The title says it all. This -previous- book from him is based on his own experience while working. The best book I found so far on this theme.

+

Further Information

The Writer

 As an executive coach for almost two decades, Francesca Giulia works with senior leaders and managers in global organizations worldwide.

Her field of expertise is personal energy management: how to sustain both performance and quality of life.

Francesca Giulia left her native Italy at the age of 19 and since then has lived and worked in various countries, such as Poland, Jordan, England, Switzerland and most recently Canada and China. She works in Italian, English, and French and is highly conversational in German and Spanish.

Her degree in Anthropology from the University of Lausanne (Switzerland), allows her coachees to benefit from both

+

theoretical and practical cross-cultural knowledge on how to lead and influence in different contexts.

She is a certified coach from Ashridge Business School (UK) and an experiential learning trainer in team building, NLP Master Practitioner, yoga teacher and is qualified in Brain Gym®, kinesiology and Qi-gong.

Some of her past and current clients include: IMD Business School, IFRC (international federation red cross), UN-Aids, Leo Pharma, COLT, STElectronics, Eli Lilly, NetWork Rail and ICC (international criminal court).

In 2012 Francesca Giulia authored: *Accedez à vos ressources,* which was published by Jouvence Editions based on her more than twenty years of experience in yoga, mindfulness and emotional intelligence. The present edition is based on the French one, but fully revised and newly illustrated.

Francesca Giulia can be contacted at: info@pem.pm

+

The Team

Even if Francesca Giulia was the *moving pen* that wrote it, the book was created through teamwork and would have been impossible without the support and expertise of these seven excellent professionals.

Claire Hellwig

Claire translated and recreated the French edition to adapt it to Anglo-Saxon sensibility. She is bilingual French/English and easily navigates the cultural subtleties of both. claire.hellwig@gmail.com

Harry van der Velde

Harry hugely increased the impact and the clarity of this book with his illustrations and made it so much more user-friendly. Indeed, one of his images is worth a thousand words.
harry@zicht.com
www.zicht.com

+

Rosa van der Velde

Rosa created an ease to navigate, visually pleasing and well structured eBook. The difference in layout between a paper book and an eBook is remarkable and it needs a lot more work than meets the eye. The layout fitted both the digital and the paper version.

rosavandervelde@gmail.com

www.rosavandervelde.com

Dennis Farrell

Dennis edited my text with great intuition and fine expertise, and provided much-needed extra energy at the last stage of this book... when I really needed it to complete this project.

A professional that I recommend.

theovernightcopywriter@gmail.com

Sundarajan Raghavan

Sundar fine tuned the layout for the printed edition and added the last touch of clarity with numerous subtle changes. He found how to enhance the book, while adapting the existing style.

An excellent creative book designer.

sundarajhan@gmail.com

Jacques Maire - founder of Jouvence Editions, believed in my very first book, and encouraged me to write a second updated edition in 2012, and so generously offered me the English rights.

The French edition of this book - which is slightly different - can be purchased online as a paperback or as a Kindle on Amazon and on www.editions-jouvence.com.

Heather Cairns Lee triggered the whole project of an English edition and gave me the confidence to move from 'thinking about it' to 'doing it'. Un grand merci, Heather!

+

Printed in Poland
by Amazon Fulfillment
Poland Sp. z o.o., Wrocław

53309521R00090